Let X=X

Let X=X

Poems by

Cleveland Wall

Cover design by Shay Culligan

ISBN: 978-1-950462-29-2

Kelsay Books Inc.

kelsaybooks.com

502 S 1040 E, A119
American Fork,Utah 84003

For Marjorie Theresa Dougherty, née Coyle

Acknowledgments

First, sincere thanks to my poet community for camaraderie, inspiration, sage advice, and the staging of as many interventions as it took to bring this book to press. (Sorry about that.) Hail and huzzah, Christopher Bursk, Joanne Leva, Patricia Goodrich, Geri Ann McLaughlin, Melinda Rizzo, Danielle Notaro, Hayden Saunier, Lorraine Henrie Lins, Elynn Alexander, Bernadette McBride, Grant Clauser, Chad Frame, Margaret Campbell, Yodi Vaden, Matt Wolf, Mauve Perle Tahat, Kailey Tedesco, Brandon Diehl, and Chloe Cole-Wilson!

Also, big, juicy thanks to Sacred Grounds Anthology, Lehigh Valley Vanguard, Transcendent Visions, Schuylkill Valley Journal, Poetry24, New Purlieu Review, Freshet, Möbius, Philadelphia Stories, Full of Crow, Petoskey Stone Press, and Voicemail Poems for picking up some of these loose pebbles and letting them shine.

Lastly, with all my heart and both my elbows, I thank my family for their extravagant support and love, especially my funny, tough, but kind kiddos Grace & Miles, and sweet Michael Wall, who is my best.

Contents

Proof

Where X is a giant oak leaf
which falls on my head as I walk
the cemetery path below, let X=X.

> Why I fasten it to my hair,
> (and is it a sign
> from O'Dochartaigh forebears,
> *People of the Oaks,*
> claiming my troubled head)

> Why I mention it to poets,
> who tell me it's good luck

> Why it becomes remote by association
> with potential augury

> :this set is null.

Let Lorenz equations express
the twist of its stem
the curl of its lobes
the air current alternately
propelling/resisting its flight

Let X! represent
the many possible outcomes
and let them have their parallel
{elsewhere} days.

The identity X=X is sufficient
to describe the moment
X has come all the way down
from its high branch to touch my crown
∴ let X=X.

0,0

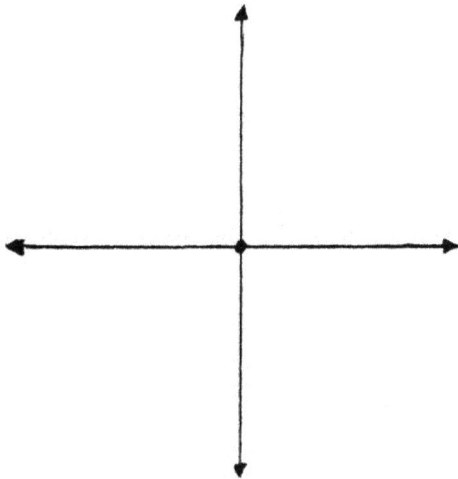

Scorpion

If your mother were a scorpion, she would let you ride
on her back for about two weeks—until you were old enough
to hunt on your own. You'd be safe under the menacing
curl of her tail, piled on amongst your many sibs,
all jockeying for purchase on her slippery exo-ribs.
After first molting, you would stay near,
stretch in your new, not yet hardened shell, not yet
fluorescent to UV. By moonlight or starlight
or whatever pale glow pulsates in the desert night,
you would all go hunting together
and see how it's done, where the prey is found
and how it's stung. You would share one
communal feast before venturing out alone.

A Likely Lad

My mother thought me a likely lad
but I was born a girl and grew
unlikelier with every year.

So, not a junior engineer
and sadly lacking the gift of gab
but pretty, she thought, and polite.

Perhaps a nice old-fashioned girl?
Not quite. I would rather be
ruthless queen, paleontologist, nun,

or none of the above. Nothing
practical, certainly. Woolgatherer,
circle squarer. At last, my ways

skewing ever more outlandish,
my mother wondered aloud
if I could really be her child at all.

Whereat I said *her* child was likely
in the royal house of Romania now,
a dreadful mix-up having occurred

all those years ago. He'd be
making the most of it, no doubt—
hail-fellow-well-met and strangely fair.

Not like me, pettishly tugging
a sable about my shoulders, repairing
to my cabinet to lounge or smoke.

When she tells this story, my mother
never fails to omit the part
where *she* suggests my unbelonging.

It does look bad and unmotherly of her.
But she likes the story, because in it
she has a child in some royal house.

True, he is hypothetical, a projection
from the mind of a problematic daughter.
But still—what a lad, eh? What a lad!

Anthony

"Anthony" my dad would call me
when I chortled with glee at the solution
to an algebra problem. I would seek
the oracle in his enormous recliner, white light
glancing up off sheaves of technical papers in his lap,
bifocals low-slung and lambent on his large nose,
Cross pen in his pocket for crosswords.

"Alright, Anthony," he would say and I hoped
the likeness was true. Anthony worked
in Dad's division at the research institute.
Brilliant but socially maladroit, he, too,
would laugh out loud upon sudden understanding,
or at any daft proposition—no matter whose.

I met him once at the office; his shirt
was inordinately green. My dad was colorblind
but his business attire was correct:
the shirt pale, the suit grey or navy.
He was known for his imperturbability.

But I could perturb him without even trying—
by taking an hour to do the dishes; by wearing
a cowled serape indoors, which was bothersome
on at least three counts;
by eating all of my peas first,
then the steak,
then the potatoes;
by humming random notes and insisting
it *was* a tune.

These trifling quirks enraged him so
that he went freakish himself in his ire
at my freakishness—this man

20

at whom colleagues marveled for his equanimity
in dealing with a professional nemesis.
However hostile the man became,
not a hair would my father turn,
but answered the more cordially. He admitted
he enjoyed infuriating the fellow in this way.

I ran into Anthony years later in the hospital,
when Dad was in for his umpteenth procedure
and Anthony, likewise, trundled an I.V. stand.
He was radiant, his hospital gown
macerated to gossamer. He told me
he'd always admired my dad for
his fair-mindedness and I laughed as I would
at any daft thing, as if I suddenly understood.

The Dictionary in My Head

is unabridged and illustrated,
fits but awkwardly, and makes my hat
sit funny on my head. My dictionary
is full of qualifiers:

>   not only,
but also   and even if   but only when
and not unless   because if so
        then only after   and otherwise,
                absolutely not!

The dictionary
                in my head is unaccredited—
rife with suspicious portmanteaux,
        words in beta, unstable verbings,
off-label usages.

But, oh, my heart—
                my heart is a grammar,
a grimoire in which all potentials are real
and the language of birds a beaky truth
keen enough to draw blood.

Delayed Gratification

In the experiment
children were given
a marshmallow each
and promised another
if they could wait.
Now tasted better
to some than *two*—
the whole pillowy mass
filling their mouths
at once, soft but resistant,
dense with couched air.
The study followed
to see who succeeded.
To no one's surprise,
the patient ones
ended up with more
in life as in the lab.
I ate my marshmallow early
and now am hungry,
but not for marshmallows.
What else have you got
behind your two-way
mirror, Doctor?

Soirée

for Mooshka

The blood bank questions
have you ever. I'm back
at that flat we shared
on McAllister. Party lights

on a scrim of swirling smoke
(cannabis, opium), glittering
cocktails; my hair done up in one
of your contraptions with flowers

—luscious, fragrant flowers—
a further intoxicant. I roll
into the kitchen on black skates
with wooden wheels.

Well before the diagnosis: you
handsome, haunted; I
ankle-deep in eyeball.
You cut yourself opening

a bottle; a bead blooms
on your fingertip—single
pomegranate seed I want
to taste, but no—you snatch it

from my mouth. No!
You will not let me
have what you have.
On my wedding day

you arise early and go downtown
for flowers, fix my hair
with blood-red velvet
and three sweet gardenias.

Scents and Sensibility

O checkout boy, I would have told you
you smell like candy, did I not fear that remark
might be misconstrued in some horrifying way.

O girl from sangha who is going away
with a new love, we embraced twice goodbye
and you left a trace of lilies of the valley,

breath of May in October. O woman
at church who smells like real roses,
I know your perfume better than I know you.

Old college friend, you liked the idea of Joy,
the costliest perfume in the world
but the odors I most associate with you

are kimchi and moth balls. O poet friend
whose scent I carried home in my hair,
this poem is my way of saying I love that

fragrance you wear—cool, dry, bitter
like some dark, woody root twisting
underground. All night I kept

bringing my hair around under my nose
trying to solve the mystery of it
and the next day, it was still there.

I am timid. I know that manners forbid
noticing the scent of another. But in poems
one may break taboo and say,

for instance, I still have the sweatshirt
you left me that smells like you
and gives me a pang for the girl I was,

capable of such a crush. I used to breathe
that bouquet like ether. You wrote me about
the bus to University, how you were sozzled

on the shampoo vapors of morning girls
fresh from their showers. I fell asleep every night
with your name on my lips. Imagine that.

Mysteries of the Colony

I work in a windowless warehouse full of documents
and one part smells unaccountably of cardamom.
Is it angels? I have heard
they can manifest as sweet perfume.

*

We store and process vehicle titles. I'm in releases.
All day I sign off liens—like loosing the tethers
on a zeppelin, as I imagine it—but nothing rises.

*

There is a pond nearby with bronze herons
in the reeds in case no real birds come,
or maybe to designate its purpose.

*

The titles have colorful scrollwork
and watermarks. You can tell by the edge
where they hail from. I have my favorites.

*

I am visited by names of beloved poets:
Thomas Hood on a Texas title, Elizabeth Bishop
on a Maryland doc—should have been a sea-going
vessel—but the shrimp-pink suits her.

*

I never knew how wrong I could be until
I came to this place, where every error is
meticulously recorded and brought to my attention.

*

I am glad today, for the moss-green paperclip
has returned to me—color that glows
in dark forest understory, confederate of trees.

*

I hear a faint music—the fellow in the next cubicle
humming a Gregorian tune. I have seen him
in the lunch room saying grace over his sandwich.

*

The place is dusty, thus the frequent sneezes
and answering chorus of blessings.
I, an unbeliever, cannot join in, though I do hope
no one's soul flies out of her body & gets lost.

*

The Keeper of Errors is pitiless in that way
of pretty young women. I know by the clack of her flats
when she is coming, and it fills me with dread.

*

In the file vault the numbered folders are
color-coded. We acquire a false
synesthesia. Pink means zero here.

*

Always some part of my attention is withheld,
a modicum of self kept back
to record the ordeal for later.

*

I picnic at the pond nearby; I lie
on my blanket under sycamores,
glad of their oxygen breath.

*

It is Tyrone who smells like cardamom.
Tyrone, the intermittent temp. I have figured it out,
for when he was here—cardamom
and when he was gone—none.

*

Seven is dark blue—"as you would expect,"
I want to say, having so absorbed
the arbitrary signifiers.

*

I release the lien and nothing rises. The title goes
in an envelope with a single wing. If it's bound
for collections, I breathe godspeed to the owner.

*

I dreamt the Keeper of Errors was knocking on the door
across the street—a social call, no cause for panic.
Still, I was glad she didn't see me.

*

On the way to lunch what looks to be a glitch
in time-space is, in fact, a small black butterfly
hovering outside the smoked glass.

*

I am glad today for a whole batch of Maryland,
shrimp-pink with a silken tooth—how it grips
the ballpoint—a tactile pleasure to sign!

*

I begin to meet myself looping back. Here
is a title I signed off last November with my full name.
I sign C Wall now; it's quicker. C Wall by name,
but not by nature. I have eroded.

*

Again the moss-green paperclip comes
with its humid giddiness! Even though the green
is latex and its confederates pulped and milled
to white rectangles. I live in the world of forms.

*

Each minute is accounted for, ascribed
its useful task, lest one go missing
or go to waste. I jam my thoughts in
edgewise; they don't really fit.

*

Robert Smith appears with some regularity,
wild hair and wonky lipstick conjured
by the name on a title and he & I go laughing
momentarily down some rural highway.

*

I am glad today for this freshly inked stamper,
spring-wound to rebound with official zeal,
its mark stark, incontrovertible.

*

The clacking shoes approach. I hold my breath
until they pass, on whatever fell errand takes them.

*

Beyond seven is lavender, of course, starlight
emerging from night sky. Nine is entropy brown.
There is nowhere else to go.

*

Everything about this place is censure. I think
I must have erred grievously to have landed here.

*

Sometimes my hair smells like amber, sometimes
nutmeg, and I don't know why.
My angel is an intermittent temp.

*

Incredibly, no one else lunches at the pond. I am glad
to have it to myself. Myself and the Canada geese,
some manky mallards, and the occasional egret.

*

It is a pleasure, I confess, to tear along the perforated line
when the buck slip comes clean away with one
flick of the wrist, the crisp severance like a little gasp!

33

*

My neighbor is humming again. It soothes me
with a monastery calm. We could be clerics
in adjacent cells, or bees—diligent, endangered,
yet ever humming an ode to that which is sweet.

*

I hoard it in the bottom of my tray, the moss-
green paperclip, and savor it for weeks. Today
I send it forth on a storm blue New Mexico title,
moss transmuted to early spring leaf.

*

Signed and stamped the titles float momentarily free.
If they rose on singular wings and burst through
the loading dock into clear air,
I am sure the pond birds would point them homeward.

*

The job is full time, but pays about half a living.
In the national style, production rises
while wages stay tethered to a bottom line.

*

When a colony collapses, all the honey goes to ruin.

*

We are urged to report errors to the Keeper,
that she might instruct the offender, but mostly we do not.
Mostly we forgive and are forgiven.

*

After lunch I walk back along the top of the berm.
There are cushiony needles under the pines.
I anoint my forehead with a touch of sap,
secret protection from the drudgery.

*

If the titles broke free, surely their vehicles would sense it
and disaffiliate themselves from garage or boatslip—
take to the open road, the open sea. They would go
just to be going, nowhere bound.

Elizabeth, My Other

*Indeed, the German folk belief was that the Doppelgänger
was a harbinger of death.*
                    —Oxford Companion to the Mind

Elizabeth used to range around Santa Cruz a step ahead
or behind me—off to one side. I'd catch a glimpse
if I turned my head quickly. Or she'd speed off
up the coast road in an old red deux chevaux.
I'd see it through the battered bus window
shrinking into the distance as we made the turn
into campus, dry gold grass barely stirring, soft-
eyed cows cooling in the shade of a few live oaks.

I know she was called Elizabeth because people
mistook us, called me by her name. Wasn't I
the girl from the party or the DK's show? No.
Even my friend Kischka, when I first met her,
imagined I had this fantastic social life
on the other side of campus. That had to be
Elizabeth. I guess I envied her,
but also she gave me the creeps.

The one time I cut my hair and it somehow
came out perfect, there she was looking
back at me from the mirror, satisfied, unsurprised,
and it froke me out. Clearly one of us had to go,
but if it were put to a vote I couldn't be sure
I wouldn't vote for her myself, she was just
that winning, my terror of meeting her in person
always spiked with a dram of longing. And I wondered
if she knew about me. Did people ask her,
Was that you dawdling down the meadow path?
Swinging in the Salvation Army yard after hours?

36

I had this cottage apartment in Beach Flats.
A footstep on the stair could be a caller
for the neighbor—we shared a porch—
but the creak of the screen door meant
the knock would be for me. Dreadful, that
palpable unknown stood outside, knuckles poised—
I would scream preemptively, in case it was
Elizabeth. Walking home at night I thought:
Was that a red car at the corner?
Was that a movement behind the curtain
of my bedroom window? What will happen
when I creak open the screen door? Those nights
I mounted the stairs slowly and stood
in the dark of the porch, listening.

Tiffin

Every day at 4 o'clock
my mother makes a cup of tea.
And it must be strong; it must
be made with boiling water
to be worth the drinking.

Every day when Dad was alive
she'd ask him if he'd like
a cup of tea and he'd say no,
often adding, "I wouldn't thank you
for a cup of tea, unless
there were something to eat with it."
Something savory he meant,
for there was always a sweet.

This was their daily ritual,
psalm and response. But the day
she asked him and he said "Sure,"
neither betrayed the least surprise,
so perhaps it had been
a fair question all along.

Conspiracy

I lie to myself with clocks.
I make them say
"It's later than you think!"
then half believe it,
let them hustle me
out the door to arrive almost
on time—less late, anyhow,
than if I lived on real time.
Real time trips me up.
The cognitive delay between
happening and experience
of happening means it
is always later than you think.
I want to hedge, pretend
the time has come
before it has. Before anything
is truly irreversible, I play at
will I won't I will I won't…
I lie to myself with clocks
that say it's later than I think
but say it with a wink;
for when they strike 13—
wrong, wrong, wrong, wrong,
wrong, wrong, wrong, wrong,
wrong, wrong, wrong, wrong,
wrong—
we all know
what time it is really.

I Never Think about The Bomb

and it's not because
I live and breathe it
like language or gravity or
indoor plumbing. I think about
those things, consider
the stench and filth
of a chamber pot, the lusty
"Gardy-loo!" announcing,
perhaps too late, the flinging
of its contents into the street
below. And that *gardy-loo*
is from the French *garde de l'eau,*
which is putting it mildly.

I suppose there were always meteors,
ice ages, other evolutionary hiccups
that could spell doom; maybe
that's why this dark cloud
feels inevitable. The others
are rare and unpredictable
and above all, out of our hands,
but come to think of it, so's the bomb,
unless you're the fellow with
his finger on the button,
which mostly, you're not.

If I think about the bomb at all,
it's the kitschy stock footage of
duck and cover, mushroom cloud,
and those oh-so-futuristic
fallout shelter signs. It was
a big deal back then—
like "reefer" and rock-and-roll.

Those girls who went hysterical
over the Beatles, or whomever,
seem quaint now.

I used to at least feel frivolous
for not worrying about it.
It was important
to wring one's hands
in the secret belief that
thought mattered.
Well, the cold war's
over now, anyway.

I have idly dreamt
under looming deadlines:
"Perhaps the End of the World
will come and save me."
But, of course, it never ends
even when it ends. The *having been*
remains, like the hush of treefall
where no one's listening.

Ironing the Shirts

even though it doesn't matter
if there are wrinkles or not.
Because here is something
that can be put right. The placket
can be made to lie flat, and the collar
to stand up, and the pocket to drape
smoothly over the breast
like a pledge of allegiance. Ironing
under a bare bulb in the basement,
a flotsam of lint runs aground
at your feet. The shirt breathes
cotton steam. A small, dry patch
of order appears and lingers
even a little while after.

Slattern

My friend's husband recently figured out
that she cleans when she is angry—
an unnerving discovery, given that
their house is unfailingly spotless.
If she were a violent person, he'd be dead now
several times over. Bludgeoned.

I, too, clean when I'm angry,
but my house is a mess. Not that I lack
for suppressed rage, only it takes
such an awful lot of it
to offset my native sloth.

I am a bad housekeeper. I feel it
keenly when I visit my friend's gleaming home
and still more keenly when she visits mine
and I try but mercifully fail
to see my wretched dwelling through her eyes.

There are levels of cleanliness to which
I am frankly oblivious.
The proof of this is
that I have bought and worn second-hand shoes.

By this sign is the slattern known
and denied the Seal of Approval
so freely given to her squeamish sisters.
For there is something irredeemably slattern
in the wearing of second-hand shoes.

Funny word, *slattern,* only for women—
a word that weds untidiness
to immorality, and yes, poor housekeeping
to unhygienic footwear. It is all of a piece,
cleanliness being next to godliness and vice
versa. I suspect I am not angry enough,
which may mean I have not sacrificed enough.
If, like my friend, I had earned
a doctoral degree first, fallen farther,
I might have the requisite fury
to obliterate all this dust and clutter.

As it is, I never finished my undergrad studies,
sensing a trap at the end of the chute
even beyond the death that all completions are.
I have a horror of completion, which should
suit me well to the task. If ever I began cleaning,
I'm sure I'd never leave off.

October Ramble

Long leaves lay this way and that,
a snapshot of how they fell.
Farther on, under the bright maples,
I picked up a candy wrapper—
red, white, and blue like the political
signs all over town. Last night
was Trick-or-Treat, decreed
by the township, not All Hallow's
Eve, nor even the Eve of Halloween.
Is it the second Friday after
the first Monday before All Souls'?
I'm never sure, but it's nothing
to do with anything hallowed
anyway. I guess it is a bid
to neutralize the dead
by changing their schedule.
But the dead have no schedule.
The damp of the ground
after a night's rain calls forth
a damp of skin that corresponds
with it. Puddles mirror
half-naked limbs of trees, their
hauteur brought down to the street
in patches. The yarn of my cape
is a hellion red from days gone by
when people crocheted—probably
illegal now for environmental reasons.
The hellion red, I mean.
When it was time to turn
toward home, it rained a little,
just teasing, then warmed.
A squirrel was gnawing
something in a disgruntled way.

The small mountain to the south
was green and gold, swathed
in mist. I wanted to edit
the foreground out of it—the plastic
playground, cinderblock school,
cracker box house. It didn't work.
My son remembers a time
when his life was happier.
He's not sure what changed.
Was it when the neighbors turned
against us? When his little
playmates were instructed
to shun him? Was it before
that, even—when we moved
here from that country place
where he was chasing rabbits?
Things are expected of him now
that never were in preschool.
And some problems never quite
resolve, square roots that go on
past the decimal point forever, or
until you stop counting—
whichever comes first.

$$y = \frac{x^2}{x^3}$$

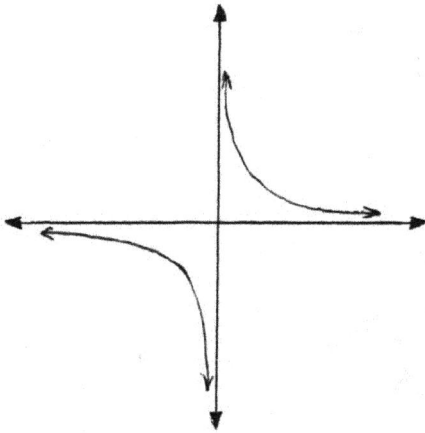

Sonnet to Consciousness

Shall I compare you to a house on fire?
Many-tongued you are, but not so frantic.
The shifting shape that animates desire
less consumptive is, but more romantic.
Shall I compare you to a railway line?
Your tracks are far more multifarious
and reaching the appointed place in time
a matter somewhat more precarious.
Whichever way I try to pin you down
the staves I use are taken from your hand
and wriggle like a Möbius strip around
my woozy brain, and sooner than I'd planned
I've fallen—Plunk!—another dreamland dupe
into the alpha and omega soup.

Drop-Out

Confessions of a Fallen Tootsie Pop

It was early on I came here, not long
after unwrapping. There was the customary
brightening, the sharpened sound, and I
was plunged into the warm dark almost
silence, save for the odd gurgle or click.
(You weren't supposed to notice those,
but we'd all heard the stories, or if not
heard, then felt them.) I remember
the knobbly weight rolling over
and over me, slicking away my edges,
taking off my outer elements easily:
meet-and-greet with saliva agents and
Whist! off they'd go down that fathomless
dark river—to where and to where
and to where? I don't know. Pure energy,
I've heard, though that's a bit
hard to imagine. I came up—three?
four times?—into the noise light,
spit-shined glossier each time,
harder and brighter—that was the prize,
supposedly: to shine as the emblem of your own
yumminess. It was all right, but then
something slipped and I lurched into space—
cool, fast, end over end; it seemed forever
till I hit—something even harder than teeth
—and I knew right then, before I stopped
rolling and came to rest
on this grate, the bond was broken.
I'd have no more truck with any
pink mouth. That world was closed. I live
in the noise light now. Sometimes the grate
rumbles. The first time it happened

I was afraid, but as no crunch ensued,
and again no crunch, I came to enjoy
those deepity tremors and the great
shuffle and flurry of new motes
that comes after. I have been
consorting with all manner of particles.
Some of them cleave to my skin;
some closer, insinuating. There is even
a kind of wet here, more subtle
than saliva. I should be sorry, maybe,
for not fulfilling the purpose my maker
intended, but I'm not. And anyway,
what good would that do? It's begun.
The ambient salts have found me.
Already tingling, I begin to swell.

Dream of the Unambitious Mermaid

My hopeless crush once asked me
"What do you dream of becoming?"
I had to pause to think it over.
I do a lot of dreaming; which,
I pondered, was my favorite?
"A mermaid in a deserted lake,"
I answered and was taken aback
when he burst out laughing.
"You can't become a mermaid!"
he said as if I didn't know that.
But what is the point of dreaming
about the possible? That's more like
planning, isn't it? "Oh, you mean
what do I plan on becoming,"
I said. I had no idea. I reckoned
I'd tend bar till I saved up enough
to travel, then travel till I ran
out of money, then tend bar...
and my plan might have worked, too,
had I not fallen in love. Anyway,
after that, my crush did not believe
I wanted him or anyone.
He spun my mermaid wish
into a siren's tale, where I'd lure
unwary boys into my waters
and drown them, fashion their bones
into furnishings for my underwater
lair. But I do not crave a bone
settee or taboret or chandelier,
however elegant. I just want to swim
in the moonlight filtering down
through lily pads and duckweed—
swim and sing and comb my long,
long and ever-tangled hair.

Getting It Wrong

The Japanese probably have a word for it,
I thought, with their knack for naming
peculiar phenomena. But I *would* think that
wouldn't I—freak that I am? I am talking about
the mistake where shared confidences
make you overconfident. You find yourself
amongst other compulsive label-peelers,
others who like the dank cellar smell,
others who can't bear to touch Styrofoam
and it is so good to be reassured by these
kindred kooks, you forget yourself
and blurt it out—the one truly oddball quirk—
say, an urge to stuff Jell-O into a stranger's ear—
that ruptures the connection and your kin
of a moment ago are suddenly horrified
to find they have been bonding
with a latent Jell-O-stuffer and you are
bathed in chagrin and alone.
Even more so than you had thought.
I described this thing to a Japanese friend
to see if he had a word for it, but he said
No. A Japanese person would not
make that mistake. Oh, I said. Right.

F O E

The forces of evil—
the forces of evil are playing croquet
and eating bonbons and you,
my friend, are far away.

The forces of evil are
poking me in the ribs and making me
drop things. They are making me
forget my lines and you, my friend—
how beautiful you were to my imagining.

The moon has slipped out of its ring,
got up to some mischief, I suppose.
The ducks are all in a row
quacking in terrible unison—
Come back! Come back!
The forces of evil have set them adrift there.
And you, my friend? And you?
You are a long time gone.

One day I shall rise up
against the wicket. But now
those forces of evil—oh they are
dazzling white, their white-picket grins
so suave none can resist them, and you,
my friend were a fabulous idea with flat feet
that padded into an ordinary house.

At the Morgan

I stalked you, Edgar, in that rich man's library
on Madison Avenue—queer place for poets to meet—
I absentee from the file vaults and you dead
superstar, your papers splayed for the curious.
Under alabaster torchères, I studied your
daguerreotype and a scrap of coffin, thinking
relic or *souvenir?* Isn't it just the sort
of trophy every fan longs to carry off,
artifact of your death, you black-clad
proto goth? The dim lights in the gallery
cast my shadow over Ulalume. My pupils
must have widened black to take in those fine
ink lines—your own dear hand, so neatly wrought—
now under the umbrage of my wooly head, its stray
hairs wandering to the margins, almost
prehensile—for what was denied my hands
was freely permitted my shadow. I confess
I swayed a little, half entranced and half
willfully silking my shadow over your page,
thinking *your* shadow must have swayed here
once and here I was dancing with that shade,
rubbing my poverty against your poverty
to mix them, to ignite them, to set the whole
rare books room alight. I eyed the guard furtively
and sidled over to The Raven, where I perched
like some relentless fowl and fairly swooned
at the metrical precision there, drunk as ever
you were on a surfeit of apple toddies. Then onward,
a foolish Fortunato, I traipsed across a disastrous
theatrical effort and some correspondence;
thence to the scroll of Doctor Tarr and Professor Fether,
a dense but tidy column. I slid down

the length of it, darkening as I went. Past
your illustrious admirers from Wilde to Kerouac
and back onto the sober January street
where, too, you must have walked. It's no use,
Eddy, I know. We will never be quits.

On the Other Side

I keep clicking my heels, but I'm still here.
What urge or demiurge propelled me hither
I don't know. I was just strolling
down some dazzled lane, when of a sudden
a tiny black funnel out by the horizon
shimmied into view, gave a wiggle,
and was gone, which had been no more
than a wisp—no more! But when again
it scritched across my path,
it was quite tall and looked
to be made of bees,
or thorny gramophone needles
or all the inky ABC's swept clean off
of all the newsprint pages now flapping
forlorn and naked against the stiles
and fence posts and silos
of some dreary outland. And again it was gone.
And I sauntered on until behind me came
a great and curious rushing. As I turned
to look about, my hair flew up
above my ears and before I knew it,
the rest of my person had lifted off,
spinning high in the whistling air
till I landed here, with a flop and a bang,
in the roiling grass under this weird sky,
a small dog nipping
at the tail twigs of my broom.

Dromomania

The sufferer was prone to wander
far from home, having forgotten who he was.
He might find himself months later
in Prague or Moscow living another life
with no recollection of traveling there.
Did he dream his real identity
while sleeping? And while awake
was he even aware of his forgetting?

The syndrome was specific to France
in the Belle Epoque, before true modernity.
How can anyone now get lost
with cameras everywhere, or walk unimpeded
across boundaries? Those days,
wide-awake dreaming was no foreign state.
The afflicted roamed like somnambulists,
and the landscape would not say them nay.

Uncertainty and the Uncollapsed Wave Function

You could be living in Mexico now
married to a snake wrangler, your morning coffee
become a ritual beyond my imagining, the water drawn
through some jury-rigged plumbing arrangement
and boiled in one of those old star-speckled enamel kettles.
It could be cowboy coffee, boiled in the water
and then carefully decanted.
Or it could be just the familiar
burble, burble, hiss of any modern drip.
How should I know? I've never been to Mexico.
You might even have gone over to instant.
Anything could happen during such a long interval.

You could be in Wyoming
on a ranch or something on that high, hard-bitten land
with a macramé owl hanging in your window
you don't even remember where it came from—
maybe a housewarming gift from some other place
you lived—the breath-fogged glass lit
by a weak-tea winter sun.

Wherever you've ended up, I'd guess it is someplace rocky.
But what do I know? Whichever way a thing was headed
when last I checked is how I imagine it carrying on
until I hear otherwise. Last time I saw you,
you were headed west and vanished into a bank
of neon swirling fog. So as far as I know,
you have lived inside the fog all this time, or else
you have continued on west across the Pacific Ocean,
and have arrived in China by now and are thriving
in that thriving new economy we keep hearing about.

Sometimes I google old friends
trying to figure out what's become of everybody,
but rarely are the results relevant. I searched for myself
and I wasn't there either, unless way out on page 37.
I didn't look that far. I searched for you
this afternoon, but the only instance
of your name was a mention on the My Space page
of somebody else who was looking for you.

I'd been reading an old journal entry in which
you lent me 10 bucks. Later, I lent you 50
which you paid back with one crisp Grant
that I kept for years, setting it aside just in case,
then finding it again upon rearranging the closets
or moving house, each time a surprise,
a smart, green time traveler smelling of leather
and that good, solid-banister scent of paper money.
I forget how I ended up spending it.
And even if I wrote it in my journal, I'd no more know
in which year or month to look for that
than I'd know where to look for you.

You could be dead,
the thought occurred to me at last.
For all I know, that very night in the fog
or later under a blistering sun
or in some linoleum kitchen
you might have come to grief. For all I know,
you are long gone from this world
and here I am still holding
your full kit of possibilities,
all uncollapsed for now,

the handsome stranger unmet,
the child unborn, the fatal collision
a mere fancy, in my mind no more likely
than your life with the snake wrangler.
Your letters of passage are all here, still valid.
I will keep them for you to spend some other day.

Powerball

It's an open window to chaos—
Come in, sweet, and presto-change me!
Against all odds, render me solvent.

It's not that I'm bad at math; I know
this will not work. But also

I know however infinitesimal, one
chance beats none, at least
by a couple of bucks' worth.

This seems absurd to those with
a sense of agency. I can't help that.

The sequence 1, 2, 3, 4, 5, 6 is
clearly improbable. Yet, twice a week
some equally far-fetched set is drawn.

So, why not mine? I buy one ticket—
only one to take me from zero
to very, very slight—and only when
the prize is inversely astronomical.

In the bargain I get a hit of hope
to last a couple days. The comedown
is rough, but while it lasts the lid lifts
from overhead and air swims in.

On a good day I forget about it,
turn my mind to the problem at hand,
hurl myself against
the problem at hand, send resumes

and applications, cover letters, thank you
notes, follow-ups and try, try again
and when my pluck runs out

I check the Powerball and if the prize
is high, I buy. The cost is low and even
losing is a kind of comfort: sometimes
things do go the way they're supposed to.

Confetti

Because the ice machine was broken
and I had to go up to the next level,
bucket under my arm, because
I was parched nigh unto death,
my achy bare feet took me past
the place where three bits of confetti
winked from the hotel hallway carpet,
three penises cut
out of chrome-finished plastic—
two pink, one silver.
And my mind wandered
to the manufacture
of penis-shaped confetti, pictured
huge industrial punches punching out
sheet after sheet of pink penises,
silver penises. Chubby, cartoonish.
Someone was in charge
of designing that silhouette.
Someone (likely else) caused a die
to be made to cut the shape out.
The many replicas were
packaged and transported
to a shop and inventoried, then sold
to a bachelorette or someone just fond
of penises, and somehow strewn
on the hotel carpet like so much
profligate seed. I put these three
strays in my pocket and carried on
in search of a functioning ice machine.

Teddy Bears

What do teddy bears do?
They make magazines.
And in these magazines
all of the ads are about
teddy bears.
But they're not really about teddy bears.

What do teddy bears want?
They want a hug.
Sometimes they dream
that they are falling, falling, always falling…
and this disturbs them.

The teddy bears, collectively, make no promises,
but they do their best because
tomorrow is another day
entirely.

When teddy bears go on holiday,
they carry no baggage.
They take no photos;
they leave no footprints.
They are like samurai.

You can't become a teddy bear
no matter how hard you try.
You can't even be "born with it"
like genius.
The teddy bears do not hold this against you.

Teddy bears are everywhere.
They are famous.
They are mostly brown.
If you see a teddy bear falling,
catch it. Hug it.
Take it to the Lost and Found.

Teddy bears are most valuable.
They make magazines
and buildings, decisions and grand schemes,
and are cuddly besides.

I had a teddy bear once,
but only for a little while.

Once I Thought I Was Wrong, but I Was Mistaken

My first pets were fish. I was keen,
named everything in the aquarium—
each fish and even the plants, Phillip and Geoffrey,
and lo! two water snails stowed away
in the foliage, a pair of gentleman callers
welcomed as accidental pets, which spawned
an infestation. Oh, but *they* were never that.
I had named them: Xavier and Ignatius.
How can a thing fall out of being once given
a name? A name will carry you
even through hell if you hold fast to it,
or so goes (blessèd, unfalsifiable) the lore.

But what of the gentle brontosaurus,
that is no more and never was?
Head of one apatosaurus, body of another,
the specious species arose not
from primordial soup but from a wishful will
to find the next big thing. We all believed
this fiction, figuring paleontologists ought to know.

And poor, demoted Pluto, once counted ninth
amongst our planets. What now of the handy
mnemonic it neatly completed? My Very Earnest Mother
Just Served Us Nine…what? Just Served Us
Nothing. Maybe I loved Pluto for its eccentricity,
skewed orbit, outlier aloofness. In retrospect,
the many anomalies should have tipped us off.
This was not one of our own stood out in left field
watching the clouds go by; it belongs to another tribe,
another class of object altogether—nothing to do with us.

Is it you I long for, my lost pets? I know you are false.
I do not love you. But I loved thinking I knew
how the stars were situated, what the bones meant,
dug up in the American west. How tiring it is
forever revising one's map of the world!
Each supplanting discovery, each step
closer to true feels more unsteady.

O my brontosaurus, my Pluto, my bonus water snails—
is it to some graveyard at the edge of town you have gone?
Are you languishing in the Kuiper belt, that junkyard
of disused forms that cool from star to rock and stand
as monuments to a lovelier reckoning of themselves?

Big Red Turtle

What is his name?
                    We do not speak it.
How do you call him, then?
                    We call him Bort.
Then that is his name.
                    No; if it were,
                    we would never use it.
Why?
                    It would be rude.
I see.
How is it spelled?
                    Why do you ask?
Just wondering.
                    It is spelled B-R-T.
No vowels.
                    No.
So it could just as well be Brat.
                    It could.
Or Ubret.
                    Exactly.
Is it Ubret?
                    No.
How can you tell
without the vowels?
                    Mm. It is hard to know.
                    That is why we say Bort.
What makes you so sure
that is not the name?
                    Because
                    he never answers to it.

The Better Part of Valor

"I am robbing you," the robber softly said,
his note a cipher to the cashier, wisp
of an impulse sketched in soft pencil,
paper rumpled soft like flannel. Sh.
"I am robbing you," he said, wavering
fuzzy on the closed circuit screen.
No sound. No overt threat.
The cashier might have slipped him
her own note: "No, you're not."
Instead, she handed over soft bills
and crisp. He went his way and after,
the manager said, "I'm sorry"
to the waiting customers.
"We must close now. We have
been robbed."

Go gently. Sh.
Go home, you seekers of snack foods
and cigarettes, and think about what
has happened and what has not.
You, sir, on your night-shift break—
put down your sandwich and go.
There is no supper for you here.
Quiet has stolen into this place—
nothing further to retail tonight.

Apothecary Dream

The street was deserted but for a cur
skulking along the wall at last light,
a sign this was no time to be abroad.
I kept to shadows, hoping
for a break in the façade, some shelter
until the scourge had passed—
whatever it was—that cowed the cur.

No lights were on in the apothecary,
but the door gave and the shop bell clanged.
Beyond the butcher paper
behind the dusty jars in the window
bright crystal bowls stood shelf upon shelf,
in each a single fish. These fish
were medicine prescribed per color and shape.

The druggist, a grayish man, soft-worn,
disordered but clean, left off
his genial arguing with the other fellow in back
when he saw me musing over the stacks
and promptly handed me
a betta, notorious fighting boy
fish whose very skin battled itself,
red striving to conquer blue and vice versa,
its billowing fins the banners
of conflicted regiments. I was to tend
this feisty chap, not as a pet—
more like a plant cultivated
for its salutary effluence of oxygen. But what
the betta would cure me of was unclear.

I had meant to bide my time here
and ponder where to go next.
Then this sudden transaction occurred
and was over so swiftly, the druggist turning
with such finality to his perennial argument
I found myself dispatched, newly saddled
with my bellicose fish in its fragile bowl.

My Rogue Self

All this effort to get a hold of myself
when my claim is tenuous at best.
All my waking hours I am constructing
this elaborate person with likes and dislikes,
ideas, idiosyncrasies—all very detailed
with a favorite Surgeon General's Warning,
favorite name of a chapter in a book
(Psychology and a Pound of Nuts).
I adopt foreign phrases, cherish irregular verbs,
prime numbers, buttons, night-blooming
jasmine, the subjunctive mood.
It is a very particular person I make
and gad about the world as and imagine
I can open and shut the blinds on her.

I am stunned afresh each time I find
she's been on walkabout without me,
like Gogol's Nose—or worse, not she,
the intended avatar, but some accidental other
who shrugs off my embellishments
without a backward glance, becomes
Tuesday Library Lady,
Brian's Kooky Little Sister, The One
With the Lemon Meringue Car,
Grilled Pastrami With Pepperoncini Black Coffee!
And these are just the ones I can guess
and don't mind mentioning in my poem
because they aren't terribly embarrassing,
maybe even endearing, because
I have already forgotten, already sunk
back into the comfy velveteen chaise longue
of imagining I have some say
in how this self is seen or not seen.

Meanwhile, there are hundreds
of rogue selves out there—I know it—
some of them foolish, some bad,
some scarcely connected with the original
overwrought farrago: just the physical image,
an extra in some stranger's dream.

There is no calling them back now
they're loose in the world. They carry on
like radio waves into space, distorting
very slowly dissipating, so along with the current
rogues there are old ones still roaming,
interfering with the new, making nodal lines
and their opposites, the convergence pattern
discernible only from a great distance.
The Girl With the Cat on Her Head and—
okay, yes, I know—The Heartless Ex,
The Worst Friend Ever.

But those aren't really me. At least,
not any more than my own fussy construct.
So when someone says,
"We were talking about you the other day"
I am doubly flummoxed. First because, yet again,
I can't fathom a notion of me existing
without my being there, furiously pedaling
the dynamo to run the generator to project
my own flickering, blinking figure
(walking round the garden, waving
to the camera). And then, since it's not
that mannered self, I wonder
which of the rogues is it this time?

74

Can I suavely like a diplomat disavow
any knowledge of her or her mission?
Probably not. The worst of it is,
these cheeky buggers, these rogues
will likely be capering about for years
after I'm gone, just as a version of
my Aunt Mary is still breathing loudly
through a mouthful of pins,
pinning a hem. I doubt it's the self
she'd have elected to survive her.
I picture them gathering over my bones
on the anniversary of my death,
all those rogues selves, and dancing
on my grave. How like them!

x=x

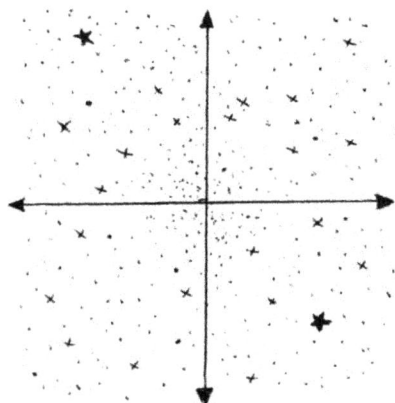

The Window of Nobody-Home

Arrived to say goodbye
to short acquaintance,
press the bell once, press it
twice. Did it ring? Surely
you heard it? Peer
through the window—
no lights inside, but the hall
mirror throws back winter
sunlight and there you are,
truncated in the glass, you
in your black coat, waiting.

Probability

But what if this coin lands on its edge?
What if a raven comes swooping in through the window and
catches it up in its beak and spirits it away to some wild place to
adorn its nest?
What if it rolls under the radiator and through that gap by the
pipes?
What if it slips through a rent in the time-space fabric and falls into
some colonial well, where it will remain an inexplicable artifact for
hundreds of years?

It could lie undiscovered in the slippery depths
or it could be hauled up and cited as proof
of devilry on the part of some hapless goody.

Maybe as it comes down the other side of its skinny arc
spinning and glittering,
I will reach out my hand and apprehend it—
put it in my pocket safe away.
Then we will have to talk.

Talk With Crow

Crow, crow, where do you go
when blacktop melts
in shimmering pools?

I bide my time at a cool lake side
become the shade of an elm.

Your black coat, crow, has soaked in
so much light it is oozing out
in the sheen of your feathers.

Yes, the colors like to preen themselves
in the daylight, but I always draw them
in again with my dark enchantments.

Are you a sorcerer, then?
Or familiar to a crone?

I am an old bird, a shadowlander.
Whatever magic I have comes from watching.

Crow, crow, what do you know?
What secret word from all your watching?

I know the sun and moon
and what lies between.

Dear crow, I have seen your colony
wheeling over the cemetery, blackening
the twilight sycamores with winter foliage.

81

We share our heat with each other
and with the naked trees.

What do you talk about
with your raucous cawing?

Listen for yourself if you want to know.
We chat about a lot of things
before tucking ourselves under night's wing.

Vade Mecum

I send you, my faraway friend, this piece of slate
from the Slate Belt—smooth, a lovely pocket stone,

ideal for skipping, though you only get to do that
once. You might carry this flat, black stone

in your pocket awaiting the perfect twilight pond
upon which to skip it, meanwhile worrying it

day to day, learning its edges, its variations
of thickness, whilst thinking what to say next, how

to express what's at the corner of your mind.
Transfer it from trouser pocket to night table to next

trouser pocket. In the dark it beams back faintest
ambient light, murmuring its persistent shape

through the night. Finger it for comfort when
everything goes pear-shaped. So small, so persistent.

Carry it month after month in the city, from interior
to interior, a plausible bit of rubble amongst heaps

of rubble parceled out in tower blocks, arrived
from everywhere, artfully placed, elastic in significance.

Burnish it with finger oils and friction; steep it
in mana; consult its contours to learn the best

argument for what you already know you want.
It could be any number of seasons before you come

to the brink—it might be dawn—of a pond so still
it summons the stone from your pocket. Will you

release it? Is this what you've waited for? Imagine
your smooth, black stone leaping unstonelike

across a pool of tenuous light, grazing the surface
lightly, then less so, touching down

at ever diminishing intervals until it is vibration,
then gone, only a ructure on the pond's skin to show

where it dipped below, its perfect destiny
married to yours, after long entanglement.

Will you be reluctant to part with this stone
or will you sidearm it boldly, give a last spin

as it leaves your fingertip to speed it on its way?
You might forget by then where it came from,

its arrival a tiny detail in your long acquaintance.
If you should throw awry, imagine the fatal, solitary

plonk, the mournful ripples echoing—
all that time together for only this. Whatever

happens will be right. You've gone so far
together already and I've not even sent it yet.

37 Birds

Cardinal, cardinal, cardinal, cardinal.
Titmouse, woodpecker, titmouse, cardinal.
(downy woodpecker)

Goose, goose, nuthatch,
cardinal, goose.

Titmouse, bluejay, nuthatch, chickadee.
Cardinal.

Goose goose goose
                    goose
            goose.

Bluejay, titmouse. Titmouse, cardinal.
Goose, goose, cardinal, goose.

Crow!
Crow, crow, crow.

Mourning dove.
Mourning dove.

And a thin crust of ice
at the edge of the pond.

16° F,
mid-January.

A Bird, Not Moving

I saw a bird not moving
on a branch in the snow
and feared the worst.

Not much stirred except
the snow falling straight
or almost straight down

till the still form resolved
into a leaf, unfallen.
Not only dead: it had
never been a bird at all.

Pas de Deux

Lanceolate the elm leaf
held on like grim death until
one February afternoon
when even pebbles cast
long shadows on the ground
the leaf let go—
frail helical blade
pirouetting in the late light
pale brown—and lucky
was I to happen along
in time for the spectacle.
It felt orchestral, the way
this leaf twirled sideways
across my path and
my bicycle momentum
rolled me past before it
could land, so I knew it
only in flight. I could
imagine the time before,
unfurling and photosynthesis,
or after, the slow relinquishing
of cellular parts to their own
next projects. I don't follow
too far those trains
of thought, though, don't
want past and future
coloring the picture with
their messy overlays,
don't want to be all
my cumbersome selves
at once instead of this
momentary office worker
pedaling home.

Tank

This is a feeder fish.
It doesn't know why
it was placed in this bare tank
with all these struggling others
and nary a plastic plant
nor a sunken ship for ambience.
Any stirrings from beyond the glass,
if noted, do not signify.
Under the tank's fibrillar fluorescent tube
the interior is bounded by mirrors
in which the already uncountable
fish are replicated many times over.
This fish that is not
pale gold like some, nor distinguished
by black spots on its tail,
this dull orange fish
in a tank full of dull orange fish
is there, and there, and there
swimming always toward
the light, the air, the food—
toward whatever boon there is
to be had from above
for its own dear sake.

Incidental Joy

Three windows open I am driving
under trees for the greeny coolth.
High summer and the old jalopy
has lost its coolant. The driver's
side window does not work.
At moderate back-road speed
the wind whips my hair up into a lather
but is soft on my skin.

I don't see the meadow but all around
a good meadow smell permeates.
Clover maybe. Or vetiver. Does that grow here?
So strong it drives me half mad
wondering what it is—
sweetgrass, honeysuckle, timothy?

Whatever it is swells like violins
frogmarching me to the feel-good conclusion
my troubles are a blessing in disguise
and even as I flare my nostrils trying
to get enough of the gorgeous air
I say No! I will not brightside this.
I do not accept this atmospheric nosegay
in lieu of a living. I don't care how *heady*!

I'm hard-bargaining as if I had a say,
but there is no intent in the rural air,
no deal on offer. The meadow sweetness
comes with the faulty car and sweltering
heat. All right, then. I'll take it.

Trouble with Poetry

Dear Mr.Collins:
I have nicked the guppies from your poem.
I didn't mean to. They probably slipped
into my stream of consciousness
and were lost in the silty mud.
I trust you will not mind.
While I was at it, I thought I'd
borrow your title as well, though not all of it.
Mustn't be greedy.

Some time after hearing your poem
I saw a tank of small fish in a pet shop,
where a girl was showing us
tetras, angelfish, pearl gouramis,
and I asked her what kind those were,
and she said, "This is a feeder fish."

Surely they had genus and species names
bestowed by impartial biologists—
maybe even a common name somewhere.
"Orange flickers" or "Throckmorton's lesser mudpuppies."
Back home they might have been
madcaps that got into the mayfly larvae
one halcyon spring. The old-timers would waggle
their dorsal fins in mock disbelief recalling it.

Notorious in their little way they may have been,
but the shop girl hadn't bothered to learn their name
any more than I bothered to learn hers
and seemed to think her answer settled the matter.
But nothing is settled with poets.

Of course I wrote a poem about them,
your too-many guppies,
now incognito as little orange feeder fish
and I was genuinely surprised
when it turned out to be a poem about me
and my brethren sub-minor poets.
We are the ones who pay to attend
poetry workshops, festivals, MFA programs.

At the Geraldine Dodge Poetry Festival,
you again read the poem, again made mention
in the green, rain-spattered tent
of a crowded fish tank startlingly like
the one in my poem.

But as you say, we are all thieves,
you and I and the other poets. So I was sure
you'd not take it amiss.
I thought to write and tell you of this
amusing irony, you who are famous for irony.
But I am not famous and have gone on
too long already for a guppy.

So instead, I make it an open letter,
and better yet, a poem!
Of which I intend, as a matter of form,
to send you a copy, of course. In your poem
you say the trouble with poetry is
that it encourages the writing of more poetry.
And here, again, is manifest proof.
But if I can deal, O Celebrated One,
then so can you.

Hydrangea Rage

Her hydrangea overhangs his garden,
blocks the sun from his tomato plants.
So he prunes the offending shrub and she
is enraged, calls him a menace—
amongst other, unmentionable things.
She is 87 years old, like Mildred,
who, when I urge her to do
the prescribed voice exercises,
tells me to fuck off, but doesn't mean it.
Saturday afternoon with Mildred,
Ms. Hydrangea's story crops up
on public radio news trivia. The incident
made national news in Britain. The neighbors
say they are fed up with the shrubbery
of ill-mannered pensioners
barging big, old-fashioned, blue heads
into other people's gardens, stealing
the very sunlight. Surely, they say,
those hydrangeas had it coming.

The Charity Dental Clinic

is strictly extraction and x-rays to see
if extraction is needed. The cavity
of two years prior is now ripe for plucking
if pain's anything to go by. Years ago

I dreamt I was a middle-aged Filipino man
with thinning hair. In the bathroom mirror
I saw my two front teeth were gone and
decided it looked OK, kind of tough.

A dream about teeth falling out
is supposed to be about humiliation.
But I was someone else losing his teeth
and he didn't mind. So why do I?

I return to the clinic and they take my wisdom
teeth with a pair of pliers under local anesthesia.
Extracted, my own teeth are deemed
a biohazard too dangerous for me to have.

I let them go and hope this scotches the headaches
that come like waves, one on top of the other.
Otherwise it's off to charity medical
to see about amputation. Is it too soon?

There is a chance of snow. Outside I wait for a ride.
Still jittery from the Novocain, jaw numb,
I suck the gauze-packed sockets, tasting blood
and something bitter meant, I guess, for healing.

Late Spring

Sometimes I fall in love
all over again on a Thursday night,
side by side on the porch, late spring,
our kids spun off
into new constellations.
The night still hums
our tune—listen, my love—
the stars are out! And just for now
there is no struggle, no ends to meet.
Only this little while around solstice
does sunset reach our room.
Earlier we were nesting spoons
in the gold light.
We had a good nap today
and tomorrow I will remember it
at odd grey moments, a secret smile
confided to the files. But tonight
we are free—undeclined infinitives:
I *to have,* you *to be.*

Love Song for My Body

My love for you is no longer
at the bottom of the pool, my love.
And as no one would have
fished it out—least of all you,
modest thing—I can only guess
it has gone amphibious, flapped
onto land on webbèd feet,
its razor gills sucking the harsh air,
searching, searching, for you—
in the rectilinear house—listen:
it wheezes below your window.
all its monster longing pitched
at your indifferent head and now
it has found the key
under the mat, for it
is a clever beast, my love
for you; it fumbles with the lock
until the bolt clicks free, crashes
through the darkened kitchen
on its way to you, my love; for you
it mounts the creaking stair.
For you it comes, all ungainly,
swaying in the doorway, your
piercing shrieks in vain; in vain
your knitting needles hurled,
the dustpan shuffle: nothing
deters my love for you.
Oh, darling—be adaptive, come
to the night lagoon. There are fish
aplenty, glittering in starlit shoals,
the beds of seaweed rocking
gently, gravity itself suspended.

Come, be buoyant, my love!
Or, if you must, faint dead away
in the creatures' arms. See
how it carries you home!

Black Walnut

You do know their roots poison everything in their paths,
don't you?

—Melinda Rizzo

Of all the magnificent trees under whose root ball
I might lie, of all places to lose my last bits of self,
poison or no, black walnut is for me,
for I love her frondy leaves,
her circumspect bark, neither too fine
nor too rough, and good for colic.
I love her high, straight bole, how the eventual branching off
is perfect cantilever for a swing. I love
the citrus tang of her green pods, their heft in hand,
thud on the ground. I love
the muscular squirrels leaping limb to limb and
the squirrels' wile and their fierce chittering
for sovereignty. I love the obdurate
shells and their brain-shaped meat. I love
dappled shade in summer, lacy silhouettes in winter. I love
how they show where the water is: by refusing to be
anywhere else. I love the satin grain of the wood,
its raveling flow revealed at last, and even
the toxicity, the loneliness, I love.
Oh, yes, black walnut—when I have grown past old,
let me weave myself in your silken stem
bite with your acerbic green
stain the fingers of late scavengers with juglone ink
drink deep through your taproot clearest water
under bedrock, under tonnage of earth
and flimsy bone cage. I will be
a kingdom of squirrels, light-eater, shape-shifter,
murderous as life!

Old Moon Goes Up

Old moon goes up,
her bandages unraveling.
Hard to believe she's whole underneath
after all that's passed here.
But her fortunes are not tied to our vicissitudes.
She shrugs and ambles on her way.

And the stones are bones that never ache.
And the stars are hearts that never break.
And blizzard flakes are wedding cakes
for earth and sky.

Old moon goes up
now steady enough
to spit in your eye—
but that's not her style.

And the snakes are charmed.
And the leaves are murmuring
from down below.
And the knowing wink belongs to the lake,
who has heard the wind whistling
these many dark nights.

Old moon goes up
bone-white and naked, but dignified.
She has cast us off and stands apart.
Oh, how we love her still!
How we yearn toward her like the tide.

The Mother of Them All

Not that I think there's a God, but if there were,
I think she is not a Him, but he is a Her.
Consider in her giddy youth how she made light
from dark, then in quick succession day and night,
earth and sky, sun and moon, land and sea,
all kinds of vegetation—flowers, fruit, a rather splendid tree—
the beasts of the field, birds of the air, bugs, rocks, and weather—
all from a standing start in six scant days, together
with the mudling seeds for an eventual throng!
Then note how her efforts flagged once the children came along
with their plaints and supplications and hosannas. ("Look at me!")
Since then we've not seen much of that fabled creativity.
Oh, she keeps her hand in—tweaking dimensions, absently messing
with quantum particles, gaps in the fossil record to keep us guessing—
but mostly she is bushed from the endless guff
of creatures who, it seems, are never loved enough
and who, despite their bumptious swagger
anent which species is the tail and which the wagger,
are really needy little mites that balk at punitude
and, thinking sooner or later to catch her in an expansive mood,
keep springing upon their poor old mother the same old test:
Why are we here, and more importantly, which do you really love best?
But having wearied once again of this behest
Dear Mother's slipped behind the stars to get some rest.

About the Author

Cleveland Wall is a poet, editor, and teaching artist in Bethlehem, PA. Her work has appeared in various journals, including *Transcendent Visions*, *Schuylkill Valley Journal*, *Poetry24*, *Freshet*, *Möbius*, *Philadelphia Stories*, *Full of Crow*, *Voicemail Poems*, and *Lehigh Valley Vanguard*, where she was resident poet for Fall 2014 and 2015.

Cleveland collaborates with her husband, Michael Wall, in the performance art project The Starry Eyes, which merges poetry with classical guitar repertoire. She is a founding member of the poetry improv group No River Twice, contributor to Lehigh Valley Poetry, a clearinghouse for community poetry events, and cohost of Tuesday Muse, a monthly poetry and music series at Bethlehem's Ice House. When not performing, Cleveland produces small-edition, handmade chapbooks, two of which have appeared in Poets House showcases.

Kelsay Books